PENGUINS
HAVE IT ALL

Li Liu

Penguins have eyes.

Penguins have heads.

3

Penguins have beaks.

Penguins have feathers.

Penguins have fish.

Penguins have flippers.

Penguins have bellies.

Penguins have feet.

Penguins have eggs.

Penguins have babies.

Penguins have penguins.

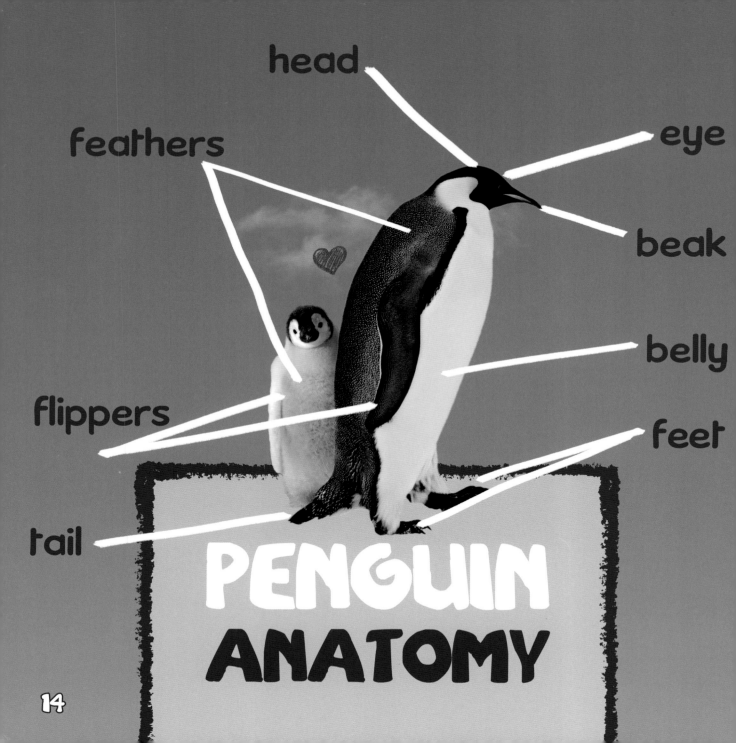

LIFE CYCLE

May

April

June–July

January–March

August

October–November

September–October

December

If you look through this book again, you'll see how penguins court other penguins. This is how penguins start a family.

I can **match** the word to the picture using the first letter sound.

fish   beaks   heads